Poems by Maiche Lev

by Maiche Lev
All Rights Reserved
Copyright © 2016 HDW Publications

This book may not be reproduced, transmitted, or stored in whole or in part by any means, including graphic, electronic, or mechanical without the express written consent of the publisher except in the case of brief quotations embodied in critical articles and reviews.

Cover and book design by David Bricker

ISBN: 978-0-9975757-0-5

For little Joey Vasquez
He listened to his mother
He spoke with his father
He followed his sister
And he snuggled with his Auntie Maria

Set List

Introduction i
Lost My Toothbrush (Shower song) 1
The Senses Don't Lie 3
Saying I 7
Speaking Circus 9
Punkin Blue Eyes 15
Will You Ever Come Over? 17
Tater Tots 21
Yeah, Dumb 27
Great Expressions 31
Water Dense, Blood Thick 33
Somethin' Else to Me 35
Spider Web Raindrop 47
Everybody Likes 51
Hey Lanois (An Imagined Conversation) 59
My Bob Dylan (In several hundred lines) 63
Oh, Atlanta 79
You Can't Dodge a Lion 83
Growin' Up (It Ain't For Kids) 87
And I Just Squeezed … 99
Texas 101
Talking Shit 105
Their Biggest Worry (Better For It) 109

Iggy Pop	113
Fierce Charter	119
Then We Can	125
Lu-Lu's Cornbread	137
100 Dollars in Miami Beach	139
Saying for Kelly Clarkson	147
Walk it Off, Sid	149
Hey, Yeah…	153
Baltimore was Closed	155
Full of Yourself	165
The Collection	171
Saying From a Prayer Book	175
Y' Know What I like About You?	177
20 Reasons NOT to go to your 30th High School Reunion	183
Let's See, a Band	187
End Notes	191

As the harmonicas whined in the loneseome nighttime
Drinking red wine as we're rolling
Many a turnin' I turn, many a lesson I learn
From followin' them dusty old fairgrounds a-callin'
             —Bob Dylan, "Dusty Old Fairgrounds"

And the circus boss leans over
Whispers in the little boy's ear
"Hey son, you wanna try the big top?"

             —Bruce Springsteen, "Wild Billy's Circus Story"

☞ *ii — Maiche Lev*

LOST MY TOOTHBRUSH
(SHOWER SONG)

Lost m' toothbrush
Uh huh
And I ain't brushed m' teeth
In 6 months time

Lost m' toothbrush
Uh huh
And I ain't brushed m' teeth
In 6 months time

Lost m' toothbrush
Uh huh
And I ain't brushed m' teeth
In 6 months time

In 6 months time
In 6 months time

Mirror
Razor
This beard's so easy t' grow

2 — Maiche Lev

Mirror

Razor

This beard's so easy t' grow

Mirror

Razor

This beard's so easy t' grow

So easy to grow

So easy to grow

I made a toothpick

Uh huh

Out've a bump on a log

I made a toothpick

Uh huh

Out've a bump on a log

I made a toothpick

Uh huh

Out've a bump on a log

A bump on a log

A bump on a log

The Senses Don't Lie

I've heard
Venice, Italy smells pretty bad
Most of the time
I've heard
Regis's blood pressure is high
From the grocery line
I've heard
What my neighbor has to say
By the bumper sticker on his car
And I've heard
It's good to get to work on time
'cause you can't kill your boss
And put his head in a jar

I've seen
Tropical sunsets
At the end of long stormy days
I've seen
Mammals killed
In the profiteer's ungodly ways
I've seen myself
In the way people talk
About seeing themselves, man

4 — *Maiche Lev*

25,000 pornographic images
At the corner bus stop stand

I've tasted
Hotdogs at Fenway Park
I've tasted
That salty lemon tequila
In dancehalls in the dark
I've tasted
Kron chocolate-covered fruit
And I've tasted
That chicory coffee
With a spoonful of beet juice

The smell of New Hampshire pine
The fragrant frangipani
From the aquatic vine
A whiff of burning spear
What d'ya feed that dog?
Get him outta here!

Oh, I've felt sad
Sad at being unworthy
Of blessings bestowed
And I've felt bad

After being hot-headed
When I could've been mellow
But I've felt good
Gaining momentum
Yes, the austerity of facing
The music.com

I've lived
And I've slept
And I've woke
And I've wondered
I've lived
And I know what it is
To pick things up
And put things asunder

I've lived and loved
And felt my trip was full
I've lived and loved
I've danced and sung
But most of all…
Mangoes rule

☞ *6 — Maiche Lev*

Saying I

The day Keith Richards dies
I'm gonna go out
And punch somebody in the face

☞ *8 — Maiche Lev*

SPEAKING CIRCUS

What comes next at the circus?
Young fan smilin' ear to ear
Stovepipe hat on the ringleader's head
Big-top tent held down tight
Rope and peg
Striped all the way from there to here
They always come this time of year

What comes next at the circus?
Clowns
Clowns in the spotlight
Brightest
They stand off
Coming to terms with the bold midgets
How many?
How many in that tiny little car can they fit?
And with their shoes so big?

There's the fancy lady in her shiny gown
Driving seven white horses around and around
Whenever they start to kick or fight
She draws her whip and y' can hear it *strike*
Standing way back
Bareback

10 — Maiche Lev

On their hind legs
Her face
Those jewels in the light
Three rings
Seven white horses
Hoofbeat sound
Around and around

What happens next at the circus?
The dark-eyed gypsies throwing knives
You think to yourself
This is how these people live their lives
I thought I was gonna pee
The flying trapeze
They sure had everyone on the edge of their seats
The Flying Zambinis!
You mean they're a family?

In the old days at the circus
All the men would gather at the Tent of the Bizarro
A well-endowed woman singing in front of a piano
Another round of some apricot Absinthe
With two drops of Sterno
The circus boss holds
The brink of control

No…
It wasn't another day at Sunday church
Sneakin' 'round the tent flap
Wide-eyed little fellas
Ladies and gentleman
Boys and girls
Welcome to the greatest show on earth
A fool is born every minute
Every minute a fool is given birth

What does the strong-man do, Daddy?
The strong-man swings the hammer that rings the bell
Daddy, how fat is the fat lady?
The fat lady is so fat
She can't find her towel

Sonny boy
What do you remember most about the show?
Tell us, Li'l Anne
How 'bout you, Mateo?
I liked the human cannonball
Yeah, in his cape and his hood!
I wasn't ready for the boom!
The human cannonball flew across the whole room!
Boom!

12 — Maiche Lev

Mattie…
Da-ad…!

What happens next at the circus?
You wouldn't think the show could ever end
A lot goes on between rings in the dark…
The big cats always need watering
Elephant prods and cummerbunds
Sequins and pushcarts
Daddy, what are those people with shovels always shovelin'?
Aren't the contortionists … *uncouth?*
It's the best getting seats near the orchestra booth

I want candy
I want popcorn
I want everything hanging there!
Ok, we'll come back when the show is over
Lights down on intermission
Let's get back to our seats
Come on
Hold hands
It's dark in there

Mateo, *now* you say you need to use the bathroom?
Oh shit…!

You popped your balloon
Dad, I lost my wallet, the one we got at Disney
Joey just pulled a tooth on his candy apple
Annie's got cotton candy in her hair
Daddy, Little Joe just slipped on an ice cream cone
I think he twisted his ankle!
Cost me 40 dollars to park my car
Had to hike halfway 'cross town with this posse t' get on out of there

What happens next at the circus?

☞ *14 — Maiche Lev*

Punkin Blue Eyes

Punkin blue eyes
Desert cacti
Coupons, good buys
Tough mama, full thighs
Good witch, no lies
Little boys' shoes'r tied

Breathless, lone sighs
Useless friends, worthless guys
Dreams full of "my oh mys"
Sickle moon, sunrise
Slipknot, family ties
Burlap blouse
Hellos, goodbyes

Rubber bands, tie dyes
Sweet nothin's, good times
Sweet Grass, Montana rollin' by
Punkin blue eyes

Crushed ice, slip-n-Slide
Hopscotch, cutie pies
Maybe you'll find

16 — Maiche Lev

Someone who blows your mind
In a Mickey Mouse tee-shirt
With nursery rhymes

Guarded, blood wise
Bygones, time flies
Good cries
Ay yi yi, yi yi, yi yi
Punkin blue eyes

WILL YOU EVER COME OVER?

Will you ever come over?
Bring some dinner
Come sit down
Take off your silly shoes
Put an album on
Walk the dogs with me
Sip some iced tea
I won't hold you down

I've got this front porch patio
But all the kids around here
Look like they're goin' to jail
We could eat key lime pie
Get some take-out from Joe's
After munching, you can sit at the drums and wail

Will y'all ever come over
Spend the day?
There's a great big pool just a stone's throw away
A huge kid's lot
Water shooting everywhere
Every which way
Lifeguards

Whistles
Zinc oxide
Hey
No running!
Little ones at Mama's side
Groovy stereo
The pool still is the place to go!

Mmmm fresh tuna subs
We could prove the world wrong
You don't have to wait a half-hour before goin' back in
That's an urban myth or something, mom

Will you ever come over
Just to see how I live?
Give me a days' notice …
Or don't
Spontaneity is…
The laundry
The floors
The bathroom
The kitchen
I don't give a good goddamn
The day you come over, that'll be bitchin'
(Dude, your microwave!)

Will you ever come over?
I wanna play with your monkey ears
I wanna crowd your face like he did
We'd be 'Reelin' in the Years'
You know that's 'Steely Dan'
'Can't Buy a Thrill'
Not 'The Royal Scam'

Will you ever come over?
Letting go
Laughter in the rain
We'd go walkin' down that country road
Not sayin' much of anything
Jilly, do your Willie Nelson imitation for me, again

☞ *20 — Maiche Lev*

Tater Tots

Tater tots
They was flash frozen
Them bad little tater tots
Fresh!
Seal's never broken

Tater tots
Hard as a rock
That's all we've got in the icebox
We'll have to go back to the spot

F' them bad little tater tots
Prized by prisoners
Good guys and bad guys
Cops and robbers.
Cowboys and Indians
Nerds and geeks and gang members
Even the dog slobbers

Tater tots
You can toast 'em
You can fry 'em
You can bake 'em in the oven

Bad little tater tots
They flash in the pan
Little chives
Little onion
I'll bring 'em when they're ready
Mama sneaks a few in the kitchen
You gotta love 'em, man
12 minutes at 375 browns 'em
Y'all get outta my kitchen now
Scram!"

Curly fries
Steak fries.
Mashed
Au gratin
Tater tots, tater tots
In the frozen section
Tater tots, tater tots
In Sheryl Crow's California mansion

French onion soup
Got its cheese and its bread
My Ore-ida tater tots got ketchup
Heinz
Red!

I could eat a plate full of 'em
And polish off a second plate, too
In a room lit by the light of a TV
"Game's on!"
This is why we do the things we do
If there ain't tater tots in Heaven
I don't know what I'll do
I just don't know what I'll do

Tater tots
Dunked
And *not dipped* in sour cream
Mmmmm
Without 'em, a man can get *mean*

Tater tots
They're in the potato family
(Duh)
Part of a well-rounded meal
You can put cheddar cheese and butter in the skin
If you can preserve the peel

Tater tots
How much can you say about 'em?
They're kinda crunchy

Kinda soft and chewy
Yes sir, tater tots
Right now
Gotta have some

Halftime
Philly and St. Louis
Hon, will you bring some more?
The Rams and Philly
You know it's bad Juju
If I don't have my crunchy chewy

Tater tots
New and improved
Extra onion
Just right
I got half a dozen boxes in my freezer
They got good shelf life

Tater tots
Oh boy, you can almost taste 'em now
Tater tots
With tater tots, things aren't quite as bad somehow
Tater tots
What a good idea

Tater tots
Yeeahhhhhh…

☞ *26 – Maiche Lev*

Yeah, Dumb

I like a woman who knows how a man is dumb
She'll lead me on in every way
Till I quiet her down some

I like a woman who knows how a man is dumb
Opens up every window
I'm going to the beach
You wanna come?

Wouldn't you like a woman who knows how a man
   is dumb?
Like a puppet show
Thumb to pinky
Pinky to thumb

A woman who knows how a man is dumb
Will take him to church
Smarten him up some

She'll cover up till she lets it show some
"And don't you step on this porch
With those muddy boots on!"

Dumb
When you come in, you take a shower, scum!
Dumb
Ok, so the score was 21 to 21….
Dumb
Narcissus, Adonis, Charles Atlas
Wheaties
Decathlons
He's her hon'

OK, son
What have you done with a lifetime of freedom?
In one way or another
We all exist in a vacuum

Dumb
I'm smart
I'm not dumb
Dumb
It was 12:00
When I realized I was havin' no fun[1]

A woman who knows how a man is dumb
She'll let the little things go
Until the hairball's spun

A woman's wisdom

Here she come

Dumb

Don't hand me no lines and keep your hands to yourself

Dumb

Doesn't he walk around all impressed with himself?

Dumb

They closed the package store and it wasn't even time

Dumb

Bury me in Uncle Ernie's Edsel '59

Honey bun, cinnebun

Dumb

Mmmm ... how about another one?

Dumb

Count from 20 backwards

First odd, then even

Dumb

Don' watch that one

Watch this one

Dumb

Too much of a good thing is usually a problem

Dumb

Don't lend your trust to any broke Bohemian

Dumb

Honey we met at the Park

Dumb

Seems like a nice person

Dumb

I didn't mean to offend anyone

Dumb

I's just usin' it as an expression

Dumb

Where have all the good times gone?

Dumb

GREAT EXPRESSIONS

Not that Dr. Lisa Wright might greet any news from me
With welcome or acceptance
But, Miss Lisa
I'm having extensive work done on my chompers down
    here in Miami
Everything I hadn't done in JAX, basically
My dentist here
I've known him since our families would get together
On different weekends and holidays
He's about 80
He compliments your work
He's a nice man, but we all know that dentists are kind
    'f twisted
You know Lisa, I too am about 80

Even if you feel that me and you are an unlikely card
And we are
We should give credence to the thought
That this heterosexual man — me
Thinks to handle your four-foot, eleven-and-a-
    half-inch
Ninety-two pound frame

32 – Maiche Lev

Yes *handle*
For hours
Quietly breathing
Still…
Motionless
Calling out to one another
Relative strangers
In a room with one candle lit

To study your face
To hear you
To breathe you in
Mountain girl
Pobrecita!

WATER DENSE, BLOOD THICK

If there was a body of water
Whose contents was drawn
   from the overall significance
Of all I've ever felt, of all I've ever seen…
You'd have a water tower so wide
It could make green all the grass
In a town the size of Abilene

Not to get too personal
But I haven't tried to picture your face for years
Not to get too personal
But I haven't tried to picture your face in years
Shakes the Clown does a pretty good Bono
Weekend in New England
Guilty pleasures

A pallet of Bibles in the galley
Of a sailboat named *Quest*
The wheel went loose
The sail went slack
The moon turned red
An Eastern star's crest

OK Nabisco
Coyote Ugly
The AMC Matador
The Rendezvous.
'Nilla wafers are best enjoyed stale
The horse says "nay-ay-ay-ay"
The cow goes "moo"

A parallel universe
Interesting … very interesting
So is the weather…
I heard "Let Love Rule" on the street last night
Worse than bombastic
And it went on forever

Now, if you could be so analytical
As to find the generic quality in almost anything…
Yes, if you could be so instantly analytical
As to find the generic quality in almost anything…
They'd say you have such a wry sense of humor
And you're smashingly good dinner company

Oh, I want to get away
I want to fly away
Yeah … yeah … yeah…

SOMETHIN' ELSE TO ME

I don't care for to hear those sounds
Music, she's something else to me
Somebody went deep inside a Pennsylvania forest
To construct this guitar for me

And those drums over there
Were carved from wood
Found in an ancient receding lake
To have a kit delivered to my house
I had to rob a bank, for Pete's sake!

I don't care for to hear those sounds
Music, she's something else to me
Reggae from the ol' school Jamaican beat
Feels like those tribes trodding through the desert
Feels like poverty's despair on the street
Tuff Gong
Old school
Ska-to-spliff
Jimmy Cliff
Peter Tosh
Zion's Lion
Bob Marley

The penny flute
The lambskin drum
That Irish dance
The balladeer raising his voice in a pub
The spirit to take a chance

Take me down to Annapolis, Maryland
That's where Danny Gatton grew up
"Cabby, 88 Elmira Street"
Unheard of technique
"Fandingus" oughtta shut 'em up

Or drop me off somewhere further north
At the exit with the giant Exxon sign
That's right; welcome to the wildest show on Earth
Where the Disciples of Soul still reign
The northeastern sound
The Drifters, the O'Jays, the Rascals
Tommy James and the Shondells
Jay and the Americans
Southside Johnny Lyons
Bruce Springsteen and the E. Street Band

Music, she's something else to me
"Superstitious"

"Cat Scratch Fever"
A song called "Sinister Minister"
"Brandy, You're a Fine Girl"
"Angie"
"Wild Horses"
"Sway" hits the ground runnin'
"Rave On"
"That'll be the Day"
"The Wreck of the Edmund Fitzgerald"
"My Ding-a-ling
"Oh, Carol"
"Jailhouse Rock"
"Garden Party"
"My Chevy Van"
"I Don't Feel Tardy"
 How many covers have been made that you wouldn't call a bastard?
"Pick Up Your China Doll; It's Only Fractured"
"American Pie"
"Ain't Your Memory Got No Pride?"
"House of the Rising Sun"
"Werewolves of London"
 I dreamed I saw a silver space ship flying in the yellow haze of the sun
 Neil Young

I don't really care for to hear those sounds
Music, she's always been something else to me
If you're gonna play in Texas
Y' gotta have a fiddle in the band
Waltz with me
123-123-123…

And the skyline of Toronto is something
   you'll get onto
But they say you've got to live there for a while[3]
I'll buy a Volkswagen bus and cruise
   British Colombus
Late summer harvest comes with a smile
I got a brand new pair of roller-skates
You got a brand new key
Dance with me, I want to be your partner
Can't you see?

Ladies and gentlemen, won't you please welcome…
This evening only…

I don't care for to hear those sounds
Music, she's always been something else to me
Ok, what it does to anyone is out 'n' out the same
They just don't write 'em like that anymore
"Fame"

"What's your name, what's your name, what's your
  name?" •*-#!^-#!
Music, somehow she's always been something else to me
Still searching for intelligence in the rock media
Circa 1973

The next U2 is as vital as the last U2
Over many a wall they've taken us — them
Bono and The Edge, Larry Mullen Jr., and
  Adam Clayton
Across many a field
Edge
Base
Drive
Spirit
A lot of love between Ireland and Great Britain

Take your syncopated dance
Take your pyrotechnics
Your spandex
Your *schtick*
Every generation puts a hero on the charts
A short time later, we cringe and laugh about it

I don't care for to hear those sounds
Music, she's something else to me

Planet Drum is a good place to start
Keep your culture
Give me F. Carlos Nakai

Tea dances
Raves
Techno-disco
Club-dub redundancies…
I don't need that much push and pull
To stir my soul
To lift my spirit
To move my body

A dollar at the door and the soda pop's free
A string of lights above a hardwood floor
I'm all cleaned up in my best blue jeans

Someone teach me how to do the two-step
Always keep a Gospel tune in the set
For Johnny, June had the table set
Hello, Jean Autry
Hello, Belle Star
Those Carter sisters keep gettin' better
   and better
And better, don't they?

I don't really care for to hear those sounds
Music's always been something else to me
Look up Mark Knopfler
Yeah, look up John Hiatt
Warren Zevon
Tom Petty

That glitter and glam sure ain't The Beatles, man
And the monsters of rock ain't The Rolling Stones
You may be a rock 'n' roll addict
Prancing on the stage
Money and drugs at your command
Women in a cage[4]

Ry Cooder
"Paris Texas"
The soundtrack to "The Border"
The Heartbreakers did "Band of the Hand"
Crimson, white, and indigo, in that order

It could be made into a monster
We'll all make a few hundred grand
Charles Mingus
The Grateful Dead
The Marshall Tucker Band

They are waiting there to sell plastic wear
The obsolete record company
The man in the suit has just bought a new car
Off the blood and the sweat and the tears of
 your dreams

Chrissy Hynde
Sheryl Crow
Patsy Klein
K.D. Lang
Emmy Lou
Shirley Cesar
Mavis Staples
Carole King
Betty Boop
Billy Holiday
Nina Simone
Aretha Franklin
Good God! Pat Benatar!
Sophie B. Hawkins
Amy Mann
Victoria Williams
Lucinda
Patty Scialfa
Deborah Harry
Helen Reddy

"Theres' got to be a morning after"
Karen Carpenter
Jane Wiedlin
Joan Osborne, too
That Mississippi girl does some *singin'!*
That Mississippi girl does some *swingin'!*

I don't care for to hear those sounds, man
Music, has always been that something else to me
"I found a diary underneath a tree
And started reading all about me"
Madam George and the Ghosts of Belfast
Bap Kennedy
Mike Scott of the Waterboys.
They sing in Ireland
Pete Townsend
The Who
Eric Clapton
(I get to write this song, man!)

Jimi Hendrix was in the Army
He ate his share of chitlins
When the lights dim twice just before the show begins
"Sunshine on my shoulders" makes me happy
"America the Beautiful"
Ray Charles' first piano lesson

And all that southern drawl can be a little too
   much, ya'll
Dorito breath and heavy metal screech
Give me steel drums and a conch shell
"Mingo Mango"
Reinhardt, Django
On a white sands beach

I just don't care to hear those sounds
Music, she's something else to me
Robert Fripp
Leo Kottke
And The Forever Man, Jim Croce

Music has always been something else to me
Talent bare and true
Something honed
Forget about me
Forget about you
Let's get lost, Chet
Like we'll never come home
The first time you heard "Free Fallin'"
Or "Freedom, No Compromise"
Came like a callin'
"Layla"

"Baker Street'"
"LA Woman"
"You Shook Me All Night Long"
Yeah, yeah, yeah "Back in Black"
The drums on "Cadillac Ranch"
The whole of "Blood on the Tracks"
"Mind Games"
"While My Guitar Gently Weeps"
"Little Wing"
"Shaft"
"Takin' it to the Streets"
"Bad to the Bone"
"Feel Like Makin' Love'
"Ode to Billie Joe"
"All You Need is Love"

I don't care for to hear those sounds
Music, she's something else to me

Well it sounds so sweet
I had to take me a chance
Rose outta my seat
Just had to dance
Started movin' my feet and clappin' my hands
And the joint was rockin' goin' 'round and 'round

A reelin' and a rockin'
What a crazy sound
And they never stopped rockin'
Till the moon went down[5]

Everybody here is outta sight
They don't bark and they don't bite
They keep things loose
They keep things light
Everybody was dancin' in the moonlight[6]
Dancin' in the moonlight...

Live at Buddakan
Live at the Palladium
Live at The Sunrise Musical Theatre
I saw Neil Sedaka rock the house at the
   Dade County Youth Fair
At the March of Dimes, K.C. and the Sunshine Band
Got an extra mile out of the people there

Vinyl to 8-track
Cassette to CD
Blueberry Hill manufactured records
Music has always been something else to me

Spider Web Raindrop

Spider web, raindrop
Raindrop, spider web
Spider web, raindrop
Raindrop, spider web

Pinecone, firelight
Firelight, pinecone
Pinecone, firelight
Firelight, pinecone

Crickets, listen
Listen, crickets
Crickets, listen
Listen, crickets

Shish-kebab, onions
Onions, shish-kebab
Shish-kebab, onions
Onions, shish-kebab

Wild boar, rattlesnake
Big bear, mountain lion
Wild boar, rattlesnake
Big bear, mountain lion

Good stick, marshmallow
Graham cracker, Hershey bar
Good stick, marshmallow
Graham cracker, Hershey bar

Tent flack, sleeping bag
Full moon, whisp'rin' wind
Tent flack, sleeping bag
Full moon, whisp'rin' wind

First light, glass lake
Glass lake, first light
First light, glass lake
Glass lake, first light

Tea bag, coffee cup
Coffee cup, tea bag
Tea bag, coffee cup
Coffee cup, tea bag

Powder milk biscuits
Buckwheat, hippy honey
Powder milk biscuits
Buckwheat, hippy honey

Dummycheck, knapsack
Knapsack, dummycheck
Dummycheck, knapsack
Knapsack, dummycheck

Helmet, double paddle
Double paddle, helmet
Helmet, double paddle
Double paddle, helmet

Spider web, raindrop
Raindrop, spider web
Spider web, raindrop
Raindrop, spider web

☞ *50 — Maiche Lev*

EVERYBODY LIKES...

Everybody likes salty scrambled eggs
Everybody likes an ice cream cone
Everybody likes those baby back ribs
They'll kill ya, but ya can't leave 'em alone

Everybody likes Bubblicious
Everybody likes Bubble Yum
Everybody likes $200
And the Captain's good rum

Everybody likes to be right
Everybody likes a nice warm bed
Everybody likes someone there to bid them goodnight
"Maybe it'll snow tomorrow and you'll get to use
    your sled"

Everybody likes a wind chime
Everybody likes to hold somebody's hand
Everybody likes "Stairway to Heaven"
I'll carry your books home if you'll help me with my
    piano again

Everybody likes to ride a skateboard
And a one-on-one game of basketball

Tide's comin' in
Wet suit and board
Surf's up. Let's go or we'll be late, y'all!

Everybody's seen a kid with a yo-yo
Sidewalk chalk!
Frisbee!
It's not just an American thing, Geppetto
An English kid kickin' a can down the street

Everybody likes a good laugh
And once in a while — it happens — a good hard cry
Oh child, if one day your world should split
   in half
It's not your job to scrape the sky

Everybody likes to take a long walk
And don't you know any fishing trip 'll do
Give a kid a reel and a rod
Teach him how to bait a hook
Soon he's walkin' from the creek
Carryin' a nice bass or two

Old folks like to take a lap around the mall
Oh yeah, both stories too!

And that sports bar always hits the spot
For the love of Mahi-Mahi
And real French onion soup

Everybody likes to put a picture in a frame
Everybody likes to hang a plant in a room
Everybody likes to take a walk through their
    old hometown
To see what feelings might arise
Down the sidewalks of their old avenue

Everybody likes the morning paper
"How 'bout them Sox?"
When Calvin and Hobbes was no more,
I sent all of my friends a special, limited edition box
(Cost me an arm and a leg)

Everybody likes "Creature Feature"
Dusty Rhodes and Soul Train
Me, I don't stop singin' in the shower,
Till my neighbors all start to complain

Everybody but *everybody* knows that water is sweet
Once you've built up a thirst
Top o' the mornin' to ya, lassie

You know I love ya more
And lass, ya know I love ya first!

Everybody can't like everything all the time
Half the people are doing something
That the other half doesn't think is at all fine
Everybody'd sure like to have saved some wasted time
Why is the grass green?
Why is the sky blue?
How does the sun shine?

Everybody'd like to belong
Everybody sure wants the floor
Nobody likes a show-off
I kinda like this class
What's your major?

Everybody likes the Air Force fly-over
Everybody likes red balloon fun
Everybody likes two all-beef patties
Special sauce, lettuce, cheese, pickles, onions on a
    sesame seed bun ... *Amen!*

Everybody likes a head of curly hair
Everybody likes James Taylor

Everybody likes autumn leaves
Horseback riding the Continental Divide
With John Belushi
Robin Williams
Christopher Reeves

Everybody likes a quality shoe
Everybody likes a warm bowl of soup
Everybody likes a bit of good news
If I won the lottery, the things I would do…

Everybody loves you, baby
There's absolutely nothin' he don't love about you
Nobody likes to be made to feel self-conscious
You haven't lived till you've put your foot into a
   Birkenstock shoe

This was gonna be a short and simple song
My dad came to the breakfast table one morn
He said he'd had a dream of children eating ice cream
On all the shores of the world
Then he asked, "Is that Kona coffee?
Son, you could write a song about that dream
It would make people happy
Good morning!
Soft-serve or sugar cone swirl"

Everybody likes a lazy day
Barefoot in blue jeans
A hot cup of tea
Curling up with a good book
To know what that means

Everybody likes a Douglas Fir
Maples in New Hampshire
Tap that syrup
We come up here for half the year
Yup
Just to have breakfast every day
In our favorite little diner

Everybody likes hardwood floors
And big French doors
A space of their own
Comfortable and clean
Everybody likes the American dream

Everybody likes to see the sunrise
Everybody likes New York City
Wouldn't everybody like to have three wives?
Johnny Cash sang "Oh, What a Pity"

Everybody likes to say
They've always stood on their own two feet
If you could do it all over again
What mistakes might you repeat?
Everybody needs shelter from the storm's winds
Nobody wins
Unless everybody wins

Everybody likes a sleepover
Everybody likes to be on top
Everybody likes a slumber party
Makin' forts and drinkin' soda pop

Everybody likes salty scrambled eggs
Everybody needs a full belly
Hey, Billy
We're goin' to the movies if it rains
There's some room in the back seat
Ask your mom
Come on over
You better hurry

☞ *58 — Maiche Lev*

Hey Lanois
(An Imagined Conversation)

Danny, I'm just kind 'f rollin' along
Hey, I've been thinking about you, man
How you doin anyway?
And I named that song, "Country Picker"
I played it fast
That's how they dance down Georgia way
Yeah, in long skirts and jeans
It's a cloggin' song
Coulda called it that too
They only do it in the high Smokies
A little in northern Texas
And I guess the southern Appalachians, too.
Feets-a-flyin'
Then louder and quicker
Crazy legs all in a line
Ya dig? It's a jigger

Yeah, Lanois
I just figured I'd call t' touch bases
Same band; different drummer
Same goofy bassist

I'm gonna catch that show on whaling next week
It's on Animal Planet … or Discovery
T.V. Worth Watching said
It was less Cousteau than "action-adventure"
Tuesady, 8:30
The reception on the bus is excellent
Oh man, the Sixers
Willie's got 'em by five in game three

Yeah, Lanois…
This cat Parker
He's built me this fandangled new guitar
It's got like a Gretsch body…
Acoustic-wide board
Herringbone
It can hold a wammy bar
What am I going to do with a wammy bar?
It's black to blonde sunburst
This guitar makes me smile
Inspiration from the first
And I read an article about the luthiers
Who built Jerry those brown wizards he played
Yeah, in *Guitar Player*
You read it, too?
You don't say

Yeah Buenos Aires
A million fuckin' two
Now I hear they're putting one on in Cuba, too
Should I call Mick or Keith?
… send em' both a Spanish-English dictionary
Dan you're too much … that's perfect

Danny…
I'm haulin' a fatboy
After that ride, had t' get *her* one
Oh, she's doin' fine
I'm as grateful as a man can be in this life
Danny, we manage to find some
They're O.K., too
She's well
No, I haven't heard from Lenina
Danny, when you installed that archway
How long did it take to get to that aqua green?
That patina?
Is it "batina" with a 'b' or "patina" with a 'p?'

Danny, you know "Oh Mercy"
It has *so* much
So much heart in the movement
And that lingering night, swampy touch

You were such a great help to me
It'll stand out
I almost feel like I couldn't get away with some of it now
"What Good Am I?"
"Most of the Time"
"Man in the Long Black Coat"

We'll hook up sometime, man
Blow a phatty…
Be good to yourself, Dan
Oh look, the Sun's come up
We're in a desert
So long, Lanois
No, no…
You're the man

My Bob Dylan
(In several hundred lines)

What's it to him?
At any given time in
That 'anything' thing?
For the wantin'
For the havin'
Glad he stepped in
Get on your travelin' shoes
If you're wanna go travelin'

What's it to him?
Farmboy Jim
Bird Dog Slim
Sweet child, little gentleman
Paying attention
Quick to question
Midwest livin'
Four seasons
Checkov by eleven
That's just how it happened
Small hometown congregation
Read those plays again
In a loft he kept himself in
Where there was more…

More nothin'
Solace to a young Bob Dylan
A brother named Alan
The Zimmermans
In one way or another
He kinda became your best friend

What's it to him?
The family came to town
And ran a theatre in Hibbington
Minnesotans
Open pit red clay iron ore mining
Second generation
American immigration
Naturalized citizens
Russian
German
Latvian/Lithuanian
Poland
England
Ellis Island.
Nineteen hundred and fourteen … or somethin'

   He's sleeping
   You'll go check the heating
   Before you head in

What's it to him?
The fabled transistor 'neath the pillow bedding
It's so bitterly cold up there
People sleep in their clothing
Radio antenna stuck in the ground somewhere
Reaching straight up and tall to the clouds
To the circling ceiling
Bewildering
Intimidating
Upward, ever upward
Lit by the moon where the needle's peaking
Befuddling
Alarming
Thunder and lightning
Disarming
Rain raining
Snow snowing
And snowing and still snowing
Until which day of the week it started
You're no longer knowing

But that antenna
The hill surrounding it there
Driving by in a '45 Pontiac, wide-eyed
There's a picture…
Kansas City

Chicago
New Orleans.
Howlin' Wolf
Muddy Waters
Albert Collins.
The Carter Sisters
Patsy Cline
One Charlie Patton
Spirituals, hymns
Blind Willie McTell
Robert Johnson
Baptist choirs
A living Mahalia Jackson
That's quite the musical education
Kids in the cold, hard school yard
Chattering about radio stations
How 'bout that new guy from Texas…?
Yeah, Willie Nelson
I heard o' him
Last night around 11:00

Bright, clear, cold northern mornings

   You look tired Bobby
   Sit down 'n' eat
   Bus'll be comin', ma

Ruth Ann's been showing me piano
It's a stand-up but she says it's a baby grand
Ruthie was laughin' so…
Her mom kept sayin', "You're too wild"
"That's enough now, children."
"Here, Bobby, take your lunch
 It's brisket and stuffing"
"Love ya each-n-every-little bit"
"Where's my hug, where's my kiss?
 Put your hat on, boykin"

What's it to him?
Chuck Berry
Little Walter
Maybelline
Jerry Lee
John Garfield
Brylcreem
Sunday school
Television
Comedians
Greasy kid's stuff, Mr. Football man
Audience participation
Laugh machine
Inner Sanctum Mysteries'
The squeakiest door ever so slowly opening

Labor Day picnics
Katherine Hepburn
Lauren Bacall
Norma Jean

   Thanks for the new sweater, Aunt Jan
   Everybody here's got the picnic spirit
   The whole clan

Death of a Salesman
Inherit the Wind
A Raisin in the Sun
Of Mice and Men

   Where've y' been?
   Been out walkin' with Ruth Ann
   Teacher caught me talkin' again
   Got a detention

Marlon Brando
Paul Newman
James Dean
Debate and chess club
Coffee and nicotine
Saturday bowlin'

"Hi Ruth Ann"
"Hi Bobby, Honey Bun"
"Wanna go smoke one?"
"I can't, I'm here with Dan"
"Where'd y' get that sweater, man?"

What's it to him?
Post industrial revolution
Post-Holocaust children
Those bobbi socks
That soda fountain
Little Richard Pennyman
New York City cool
Windows blackened
Miles Davis playin' with Lionel Hampton
When Charlie Parker took New York City
No one could pay the ransom
Jerry Lewis and the unexplained laughter of
   all Frenchmen
Hollywood was reefer, alcohol, and cocaine
Some things never change
San Francisco was once known for its opium dens
There was prohibition
Prohibition
A fine working, well made money-making machine[7]

The depression
Brooks Brothers conservatism
Roosevelt
Eisenhower
Truman
Steinbeck
Whitman, a sweaty toothed madman
Vanderbilt
Rockefeller
Chaplin
Chronological time is an overrated thing

A beat up 80cc dirt bike
Firin'
Canadian arctic skies
Fallin'
Tripped out twilights
On 10,000 lakes' reflections
A river's mirror's winding strum
Your natural surroundings
And what you become

"Ruth Ann, this jacket isn't holding me
I'm freezing"
"Ruthie, what are you doing?
That's not what I had in mind, Ruthie!"

"You shush
 Just you hush up!
 You don't know a thing"

Papa was an electrician
A handyman
A bare cement floor in a hardware store
A teenager sweepin'
Over by the scales
Around the nail bin
Reachin' up to change the radio station
Talkin' out back with a black man
Wearing an apron from the next door delicatessen
Trading questions
Laughin' about somethin'

 "Gotta get back in"
 "Me too, my young friend"

AM radio, Yeah
Little Richard tearin' it up like it'd never been
The likes of the likes of Hank Williams
That Tupelo, Mississippi guitar lesson
Buddy Holly
Rave on!
Alan Freed, again

'Payola' was just the way it was
You can't call it corruption
This was the millennia before Wolfman Jack or
   Kasey Kasem
Dick Clark wasn't even a letterman on the bandstand
Before Annette Funicello and her boyfriend
Another kind of teenage rebellion
Before Marvel Comics' back page spin
1954 and Alfred E Neuman

   "Whisky, beer, vodka, bourbon, or wine?
   Anything you can get from your father's bar 'll
      be fine"
   "Ruth Ann, she's just my other girlfriend"
   "Ante up
   You in?"

Big-eyed girls with bouncy curls and a pack of Camels
Bitchin'
Marlys
Parliaments
A first marijuana cigarette
Tight angora sweater stitchin'
Underage hang-outs way out beyond…
Beyond the back roads of the next county town
Pool tables

Neon
Hey you! Some identification?
We just come to where the music's comin' from

That's not a '49 Ford; it's a '41
Rich boys get Corvettes
And fine girls drive Mustangs
Right off the line
Let's go to the Hop and hang
Waitresses with roller skates on
Dang!
Which Danny Gatton record was that off of again?
Topo Gigio on Ed Sullivan
Mr. Ed
8 pagers
Howdy Doody
American pie
Politicians
Radio shows like 'The Prairie Home Companion"
English majors who've never spent a stoned day
Y' gotta love Garrison; y'know he's Lutheran
With a middle name like Wayne…
Another great Minnesotan

McCarthyism
The Rosenbergs

Black Cadillacs
Thin ties worn by agents
Alan and Neil Lomax
With the world's first recorded rapper's chants
Dusty, stained, raggedy shirts and pants
Three little girls at church in their Sunday best
Malcom X
"Get your hand outta my pockets"

What's it to him?
To walk a ragged mile
Knowin' y' got no friend
To wake up by the side of the road in the rain
Shiverin'
Big Bill Broonzy in the beginnin'
Learned to sing by singin' like him
Woody Guthrie
Joe Lewis
Sonny Liston.
Heddy Leddbetter
Sonnyboy Williamson
Big Joe Turner
Harpo Slim.
Professor Longhair
James Cotton
Alan Toussaint

Billy Preston
And lest we forget, Ray Charles, the piano man
And the thousand others in between

This is our tattered connection
All-great feeling, reelin' rockin'
Mens and womens
Homegrown dealin' musicians
Black men know what it is to be in society
With a shackle on your hands
The feelings endured in the 'made-to feel-lesser' person
The black child
The black woman
The dream of beauty that cannot be taken
Between the voice of Nina Simone
And Billy Holiday's grammophone
An endless dream of cigarettes and magazines
Dr. Zhivago
Gone With the Wind
The African Queen
Bessie Smith fallin' off the wagon
Circus hands and marching bands
In the middle of it all
In one cold Hibbington
A wound up young man of Semitic origins
Dealin' to himself about what it all means

What lies within…
Sixteen
Seventeen
Denim blue jeans
The empty feelings of million-to-one dreams
Pressure
Future
Career decisions
Staggerin' in

"Where y' been?"
"Just out walkin'"
"It's Wednesday, son"
"You try dear, I can't talk to him"
"End of spring is your orientation, young man
You got in; you're goin'
What are you thinkin'?"
"There's stew on the stove and bread in the oven
You must be half frozen, Bobby
Go change into somethin'!"

It was dawning on them
That with him
They were in for somethin'…
Something like his guitar

His shoes
And his thumb…

  "There he is"
  "Where?"
  "There"
  "Oh Jen … I think I saw him at orientation"
  "Hi"
  "What're you majoring in?"
  "Me? Folk singin
   But I may become a mathematician
   Or a West Coast dietician
   I been lucky before, I'll be lucky again"
  "Oh"

  "He thinks he's cool"
  "He is cool, Jen"
  "Yeah, he's got that guitar and those records by
     the dozen!"
  "Yeah, he told me he stole 'em"
  "Told me the same thing
   From a Tennessee radio station"
  "He told *me* he got them from some place in
     Kentucky…
   Cumberland"

"I hear he's half Canadian"
"Whatever; he sure is handsome"
"That's not handsome, Jen; that's *pretty*"

"He told me his name was Bob somethin'
I think he said Bob Dylan"

What's it to him?

OH, ATLANTA

I'd walk to Atlanta for a kiss
Here I am, sweetheart
You thought I was callin' from home
But the phone was right here in my gear, sweetness

I'd walk to Atlanta for a kiss
That's what romance has become to me, kind miss
Mellow as the month of May at your doorsteps
I'm in need of a shower
Everything in my sack smells like this

Getting here was half a nightmare
It was
But seeing you again I revel in purpose
Yes, my *purpose*
The thought of seeing you again kept me smilin'
Every step across the surface
Asphalt
Cement
Sidewalk
Sun and sand
I've come all this way for a kiss
Do with me what you will
I love you; don't you understand?

Y' turn nineteen when passion is easiest
When you turn twenty-nine
The fighting can get serious
In no time at all, you're thirty-six
Holdin' a bag of tricks
At forty-four, I walked to Atlanta
To give a gal a kiss

Yes, I walked the line of A1A highway
I took off my shoes to walk in the sand
I could hear the ocean over the dunes
Just a stone's throw away
"Steal away with me, mama
Crazy as I am"

There was an electrical storm, darlin'
A couple of days ago
Tree limbs crackled
Shadows hissed
What have I got myself into?
Out in the cold over this girl I've always missed

Meet me at the fountain at Emory
We'll be at five points by noon
At the top of the hostel there
I've got a charming little room

Oh I'd walk to Atlanta for a kiss
Florida
Can't find a map any kinder than this
Atlanta, Savanna
Springtime in the south
Can't wait to put a Georgia peach in my mouth

First to talk about the time gone by…
No
First … embraces
Sister, the last 100 miles was no slice of pie
But I'm singin' a new tune
Goes something like this…

Conyers was cold
Macon was mud
In Tekoa it snowed
Marietta, check come
Slept right in Waycross
Valdosta's like home
Brunswick, got a motel room
Motel room got a door
She stepped right in
Like Daisy Duke herself
Lookin' like Anaïs Nin
Baby, you'd better go

You aint' the one
It'd be a sin

I'm thinking of how it'll be
When I come to knock on your door
"Thought I'd bring you somethin' special, baby
And that'd be me
Besos, mi amor"

You Can't Dodge a Lion

You can't dodge a lion
And anyone who'd tell you different
Must be a little mixed up
You cannot dodge a lion
A lion'll swat you down
Swat you down and eat you up!

A lion comes without a sound
Four paws on the ground
450 pounds of cat pacin' 'round
Silent pounce
Silent leap
A lion…
You is his next somethin' to eat!

Ferocious is fast
Ferocious is mean
Midnight growl
Moonlight prowl
Senses sharp
Senses keen

Deep breathin'
Deep heavin'

Hot blooded roar
Eyes of fire
His mane, sire
Ripplin' musculature
King predator
Doesn't cuddle the cubs of his predecessor

Scramble
Swipe
Paws claw
Fangs maul
The "King of Beasts"
That's what he's called

Tears the flesh off of a man
Like paper from a gift
Gave entire stadiums of Romans a lift
And they fight amongst each other
Boys will be boys
All up on their hind legs
Built to survive
Built to destroy

He'll trot 20 miles
By the strength of his will
At the feeding frenzy

He's the first to get his fill
Grass and dust
Heat and lust
Fight all night
Sleep in the shade
A lion is the master of his domain

Boundary to boundary
The lion he'll strip the bark off a tree
And climb straight up if he's real hungry
I saw it on National Geographic or Discovery
Eyes peeled for a crock at the watering hole
A lion is king of the jungle…
I think I hear Tarzan's call

Don't wanna meet up with a grizzly
Don't wanna stumble on no stripes
Lions and tigers and bears, Dorothy!
Stay in the boat!
Absolutely goddamn right!

See 'em at the circus
The Las Vegas Times
No more jive, Roy
Oh, boy…
Not this time

You don't wanna run with the bulls
And you don't wanna dodge a lion
Let them say what they will
You got better things to do
Than to be a fool for tryin'
'cuz you can't dodge a lion

But since you've come all this way
To act so foolishly
You're next up
Good luck
They keep 'em hungry

No, you can't dodge a lion
And anyone who'd tell you different
Must be a little mixed up
You cannot dodge a lion
A lion'll swat you down
Swat you down and eat you up!

Growin' Up (It Ain't For Kids)

Skinned my knee
Stubbed my toe
Pulled my shoulder
Broke my nose
Split my finger
Bit my lip
Cracked a tooth
Got a chip

Growin' up
It ain't for kids

Funny bone ain't so funny
Ah, Bruce Lee fractured wrist
Major flu
Knotted head
Ankle twist
Braces
Metal mouth
Hard to smile
Tattoos
Earrings
The diabetic juvenile

Growin' up
It ain't for kids

Slipped in a puddle
Smashed my thumb
Still that one strikes me
Still it comes
Sprains and jams
Had the wind knocked out of me playin' football on muddy fields
With guys faster and bigger than I am

Growin' up
It ain't for kids

Y' get poked in the face by fingers and sticks
July 4th sparklers
Fahrenheit wicks
And your sisters, they pulled your hair and thought it was funny to make you cry
And they laughed when you got your hand stuck in the car door that time

Growin' up
It ain't for kids

And that time a fully-grown horse stepped on your
   7-year-old foot
And the horse trainer was less than completely
   sympathetic to boot
Off of your bike seat
From a full day's ride
For half the next week
Somethin' different about your stride

Growin' up
It ain't for kids

Ear infections
Burning the roof of your mouth
Lice in the 3rd grade, for God's sake
Bubblin' Bactine
Hydrogen Peroxide
Alcohol
Cotton ball
Ouch, it hurts!
Wait!
Wait!

Growin' up
It ain't for kids

Splinters
The worst!
Tweezers are the devil's tool
Cutting your cuticles too close to the quick
The anemic
Fingers pricked
After school

Growin' up
It ain't for kids

Growth pains past midnight
Ben Gay
Icy Hot
Hornets in the monkey bars
Calamine lotion against your pajama top
Fish bones hidden in that filet
Mosquitoes enough to drive you batty

Growin' up
It aint for kids

Oil-based vaccinations from hell
Booster shots and doctor visits we all remember well
Just the *taste* of penicillin

Finding out what you're allergic to...
Poison ivy
Poison oak
Peanut butter
It can happen to you!

Growin' up, it ain't for kids

Paper cuts
Electric shocks
Prickly briars in your tube socks
Never getting picked for the team
Hysterical parents
Car accidents

Growin' up
It ain't for kids

Sittin' in a red ant pile
Bad tuna fish
A mouthful of spoiled milk
Soccer field shinsplints
Charlie-horses
Rat-tails
Hammers and nails

Survival courses
The loneliness of parents' divorces

Growin' up
It ain't for kids

Thunderstorms
Deviated septums
Thermometers
Playin' hookey
Playin' possum
Kaopectate
Pepto Bismol
Robitussin
Home from school
The Price Is Right
Tall Coke
Grilled cheese
"Thanks, Mom"

Growin' up
It ain't for kids
Asthma
Bronchitis
Bug bites
Encephalitis

Those allergies—they *are* real
The "boy in the plastic bubble" deal

Growin' up
It ain't for kids

Worst thing in the world
Losing your mom at the mall
Catching a ride on the instep of your daddy's boot
Injured pride
Shaken up 'n' all
No butts!
They throw elbows
Will you please stop touching me!
Tonsillitis
Tonsillectomies

Growin' up
It ain't for kids

And Larry kicked me full force in the knee at his
    second grade birthday party
I remember Elizabeth's voice in the air
I didn't want to cry, but I did
Those brown and white patent leather little boy shoes
Stern and hardy

That wasn't nice
That wasn't fair
It's *my* party
And you can just get outta here!

Growin' up
It ain't for kids

Extreme shyness
Drug problems
Hyperactivity
One in less than a hundred kids will have some
    form of autism
It used to be one in a hundred 'n' fifty
Maybe tonight I'll read
And turn off the blessed TV
Teenage depression
Multiple abortions
Christ, suicide pacts
Punk anarchy

Growin' up
It ain't for kids
Kids go around punching each other in the arm as
    hard as they can
They play basketball

And suffer the most painful thing in the universe
   known to man:
Basketball finger jams
Not again!
Ohhh!

Growin' up
It ain't for kids

Cross-country coach
Gettin' the most out of his team
Cramps on cramps
Summertime steam
Muscle spasms
Gutbusters
Suckin' wind
Heat stroke
Delirium

To the beach
The beach is fun
Hot sand!
Hot sand!
Singed eyes
Singed ears
Portuguese man-a-war

Deep tan
The lifeguard can't find his nutmeg
No one's got any ice
The beach is fun
Got its own undertow, riptides, and sea lice

Growin' up
It ain't for kids

Back to the dentist
Poking around for cavities.
Novocain shot
"One?"
"No. Two, please"
Bite down on this and we'll take an X-ray
A drill that's shrill
Here's your next appointment…
And a lollipop
Take care of your teeth
Have a nice day

Growin' up
It ain't for kids
Skinned my knee
Stubbed my toe
Pulled my shoulder

Broke my nose
Split my finger
Bit my lip
Cracked a tooth
Got a chip

Growin' up
It ain't for kids

98 — Maiche Lev

And I Just Squeezed…

And I just squeezed a whole thing of lighter fluid
On the loudest bike on the street
All over the grill and the pipes
But not a drop on the seat
I wonder how loud he's gonna be
When the residue meets the heat
Son of a bitch wakes up every soul in
   the neighbourhood
Every time he goes down the street

Fifty-seven thousand lightning strikes reached
   the ground
In the French vineyards where the grapes grew
My favourite porn star was named something like
Desiree Dominesque
But *shhhh*
The next-door neighbors will know
That you figured out how to
Work the box and order a show

The homeless at night in Miami
They're dust covered … rust covered
Sleepin' in the storefront
There's fresh food in the dumpster

Of the Italian restaurant
You can improve their situation
What of the will to be well?
Here's a little kitty to take care of
We're here to help; this isn't a cell

Rainy days are for guys with guitars
Who know how hard it is
Time waits for no one
And ain't I been jus' about my business?

I didn't put any petroleum
On that cat's motorbike
I'm sure he's a real congenial dude
Someone we'd all probably like
Unaware of the nuisance he's become
I think I hear him
A yellow Harley Davidson
Yep
Here he come
Red pinstripe stylin'
Gettin' on four in the morning
What can be done?

Texas

Texas, it's a travelin' show
Texas, a boy at a rodeo
Texas, state of the lone star
Texas, you can't ask f' more
You can't get too far away from…

Texas, it's like a whole other country
In Texas, goddamn; everything's free
Texas, a Louisiana Saturday night
Mobile, Valdosta, Ocala, Alright!

Texas, yippy-cay-ye-o, chubby truckers
Texas, we are the dustbowl cornhuskers
Texas, cotton dress, southern bell, magnolia love
Two-tone angels, will meet you at the bayou—
   borderline of…

Texas
Remember the Alamo
Texas, "What's that you say, pardner?"
"Which way did he go?"
Texas—Abbott, Texas, home of Mr. Willie Nelson
Janis Joplin, Poncho and Lefty, Lyle Lovett,
And that good lookin' man, Chris Christopherson

Texas, ZZ Top
Texas, yellow onion crop
Texas, "Crystal, won't you please pass the jelly?"
Don't wanna mention no soap opera stars in the
   same sentence as Buddy Holly

Texas, Governor Anne
Texas, Southern Man
Texas, Houston, Dallas, Austin
Good God! Those cheerleaders in Cowboy Stadium

Texas, 6th Street
Texas, oh, the places you'll go
The people you'll meet in Texas
Sure do like that Stetson hat
Skinny Charlie Sexton playin' a stiff black
   Fender Strat

Texas, an Electric Ladyland shopping spree
Texas, Kinky Friedman (Who's he?)
Texas, High Plains Drifters
Texas, got me a new pair o' rattlesnake shitkickers

Texas, it's a travelin' show
Texas, a kid at the rodeo

Texas, the Lone Star State
Texas, the getaways must be great
From Texas!
Texas!
Don't mess with Texas!

Talking Shit

The shit if I know
Holy shit!
Shit, man!
Fuckin' shit
Fuckin' shit, man
Talking shit
Shit for brains
Shit faced
Getting shitfaced
Getting shitfaced again
My ex-wife used to say that mysterious people were
　usually full of shit
Shit outta luck
Isn't that some shit?
Are you shittin' me?
I read the shit you wrote about me in your book, man
I don't give a shit
I don't give a shit anymore
That's what I keep having to remind myself of
That kind of shit
Everything you touch turns to shit
You're not really gonna hand me that shit again?
Horse shit

Bullshit

Cow shit

Boy, you're gonna clean up all that shit. Right?

This is bullshit!

I shit you not

You're shittin' me

I shit you *not!*

Moving away was the only thing that got me off the shit

Hey, check your sneaks

Who stepped in shit?

It's all the same shit

Can you believe this shit?

Well … shit

That's bullshit

A '76 Stingray Corvette, dark blue, black leather interior

That's the shit

Stadium shows are usually pretty shitty

You look like shit

Fuck that shit

When the shit hits the fan…

They just kept pilin' on more shit

I didn't write 'em for that, but I figured, "shit …"[8]

Oh shit!

People aren't deserving of all that shit
Christ, some people ain't got shit
I'm hungry as shit
You're a fat shit
Aaawwww… shit cakes!
Shee-itt, *ruuuun!*
They had no idea what kind've shit was about t' go down
Heavy shit
That's some heavy shit
If it looks like shit and it smells like shit…
In *The Gumball Rally,* Raul Julia was cool as shit
And wasn't he the shit in those *Munsters* remakes, too?
My shit's fucked up
Cut the crap
Cut the shit
I don't give a shit and you don't give a shit, either
One thing about turning gray prematurely:
Middle-aged divorcees check out your shit
Shit man, she's rich…
Roeder used to say, if y' asked him
"Life is like digging through shit to find a diamond
And, LSD was like digging through diamonds
Only to find shit"
Have a nice day … y' little shit!
In Canarsie, they call each other "little shits"

Does a bear shit in the woods?
If y' can't shit, get off the pot
Your name is mud, and you're up shit's creek
When will he be through with this shit?

I pooped today

Their Biggest Worry
(Better For It)

Their biggest worry
Was whether or not they had drum skins
Their only thought
Was what kind of skins the music store had in

Greatness is anywhere
Anywhere in time
What amusement be yours
What amusement be mine

A Chinese child smiling
At the first bow on a violin
That John Denver song
That brings tears to the eyes of all Americans

Greatness is anywhere
Anywhere in time
What amusement be yours
What amusement be mine

Doesn't Bonnie Raitt have the best dimples?
Leaning back behind her guitar
Smilin' playing slide

Makes it look so simple
Makes you wanna get in your car
And go to the music store and *buy*
Bonnie Raitt doesn't hide

Greatness is anywhere
Anywhere in time
What amusement be yours
What amusement be mine

Old school
New sounds
Get back to where you once belonged
Go away, and don't come back
Till you got a couple o' decent songs

Blood, sweat, and tears
Can't fit enough into all these years
Blood, sweat, and muscle
From morning till night
All y' ever do is hustle[9]

Greatness is anywhere
Anywhere in time
What amusement be yours
What amusement be thine

You know that scene in the Johnny Cash movie
When Elvis speaks to Johnny about June
Upstairs in the shadowed rafters?
She was doin' that when you and me
Were still ridin' our daddy's boot
Not much outta diapers

Clawing to get to the tops of their fields
Every clashing speciality
I had a great place to blow my harp
Good echo under the big bridge over Biscayne Bay

I was at a bluegrass festival
It was on the third day
This little kid comes up to me and begins to play
He played everything y' ever knew
Upside down 'n' inside out
I turned to him and I said
"Kid, you is what it's all about"
Greatness is…

Iggy Pop

Iggy Pop, man
Iggy Pop
The one who don't know when to stop
He hit the charts but never the top

Iggy Pop, man
Iggy Pop
Voice so low
The floor got mopped
Seen 'im in a long white Caprice
Whale of a ragtop
Straw hat on his head
Shoulder-length crop
And I think I spotted him once
In a greasy Cuban restaurant

Iggy Pop, man
Iggy Pop
If he's got a greatest hits album
That's the last place to start
I'm not exactly sure what I mean by that
But then maybe I do…
He plays from the heart

Iggy Pop, man
Iggy Pop
Zevon, Lou Reed, The Cars
That rock
Chrissie Hynde with The Pretenders
New wave chic
Heroine, cocaine, rail-thin
That lot
Bowie, Blondie
Lookin' ready to drop

Iggy Pop, man
Iggy Pop
Lives with his old lady
Down past Simpson Park
His cat must meow
And his dog prob'ly bark
My friend says he's got a sporty sailboat
At the marina by the cut
"Ladies are 'unwell'; gentlemen vomit!"[10]

Iggy Pop, man
Iggy Pop
You can ask Jakob
You can ask Adam

He's the coolest living soul
On the planet
Iggy Pop
They all dig 'im

Iggy Pop, man
Iggy Pop
I know *this* many Dylan songs
I know 'em flat man, from the top
I could come over and we could
Sing 'em and sing 'em
I'll blow some harp
You play rhythm
How 'bout "Lily, Rosemary, and the Jack of Hearts?"

Iggy Pop, man
Iggy Pop
We'll go out for Argentinian chops
In that big Chevy ragtop
I know it's your Caprice Classic
Iggy Pop's my friend
Ain't that fantastic?

Iggy Pop, man
Iggy Pop

When he was seven years old
His sisters skipped babysitting
And went to the hop
Little Iggy in the middle
Motor City Motown
Where the music never stops

Iggy Pop, man
Iggy Pop
Never buttons his shirt
Bottom to top
The Crash Test Dummies, the Psychedelic Furs
Courtney Love
Iggy Pop and The Verve

Iggy Pop, man
Iggy Pop
He digs his fans
And fans he's got
In a second, they'll sing you one of his songs
Then they'll turn
And laugh it off

Iggy Pop, man
Iggy Pop

I should rattle off a bunch of his tunes
But…
But I made all this up
I don't know a thing about Iggy Pop…
I know Linda Ronstadt
Ann Murray's my date
I'm homespun like that

But Iggy Pop, man
Iggy Pop
Man, that guy felt the *need* to go over the top
Yeah, like a stooge who never knows when to stop

Iggy Pop, man
Iggy Pop
He's the guy at the party
Who don't get up at all
But at the stroke of midnight
He changes into a sombrero
And walks bare-assed through the ball

Iggy Pop, man
Iggy Pop,
A little bit of this'll get you up
A little bit of that'll get you down

He took William S. Burroughs out to lunch
Paper said this guitar man
Shows you how it's done

Iggy Pop, man
Iggy Pop

Fierce Charter

Fierce charter
Wade in the water
Salty dog ambition
Bonfires
Skin suits
Rods for fishin'
Husqvarna
Carving up the continental coast
Filipino box spring Guam spit-roast
Seems a common way to go
Anchor, ship-to-shore
A fierce charter

"I think I'll have the Hudson River rainbow trout
And the Louisiana Rain Mint Julep ice tea"
"Fine choice, sir
May I suggest the giant Andalusian escargot?
It's one of our specialties"
And if we never did have the real thing
Passionate kisses
Wall-to-wall on the living room floor
Still, we were automatic for the people
Yes we were
A fierce charter

Whispers in the slack tide glass
Close your eyes
You won't smell of fear, alas
Set your clock to times you won't end up feeling robbed, son
Rhythm…
Sunshine soon come
You'll differentiate yourself by and by
You'll never know your own age
The young at heart stay young at heart
Protect the sternum
And regions below the ribcage
Snorkel and mask
Flippers and spear
We never swim without a partner 'round here
"On deck!"
  "Look alive, sailors!"
A fierce charter

It's Fleet Week in Turkey
Fragrant hashish in the air
The coffee is sweet
Black and murky
Don't walk alone
And don't linger in there
We'll refuel

Shop supplies and groceries
Conceal every inch of your body
Always past your knees
Levi needs strings
Find out what gauge he needs
We need *Grand Marnier*
Status quo
We'll leave when the day starts getting darker
Fierce charter

It wasn't just a blackbird
It was a raven
Large and muscular
'tween the next piling and our slip
Like the sound of a good sized flag unfurling
It *whipped* itself right off the top
And flew away, it did
Do-re-me-fa-so-la-ti-do
The Northwest Passage
Permafrost
East of Prudhoe
Teak on the floor
Turbine powered
An 80-foot dragon goin' 95 miles an hour
Quebec to Miami in under 36 hours
A fierce charter

Fierce charter
Wade in the water
Salty dog ambition
Bonfires
Skin suits
Rods for fishin'
I've heard that the Magellan Straits way down
 South have whirlpools
They say don't turn your back on the sea
Like anything that doesn't suffer fools
Pirates who would not hesitate
To make a crew into martyrs
They come to make theirs
Anything you call yours
Throttle man
Driver
Navigator
A weapon in a retractable turret of surprisingly
 high caliber
Arrivederci
Adieu
Andiamo
See you later
We go to go
We run to run
Kevlar

Magnum
Heavy
McDonnell Douglas
Aronow
Donzi
Cigarette
Fountain
Formula
Thunderboat Row
Katrin Theodoli

Like there's something we're after
Chasing the moon
Racing the sun
Farther
Faster
Yeah, like there's something we're after…

A fierce charter

Then We Can

Then we can get the window fixed in the car
Then we can get a whole handful
Of jellybeans out of the jar

Then someone else can pick up the kid
We could get away honey
Euros convert nicely into English quid

Then they could all go to camp
In the woods of Maine
Every day will be one game
After another game

Then everything will be different
But nothing will have changed
Then we will have learned
To sit back and complain

Jellybeans…
Poof!
We could buy the whole store
Then we wouldn't have to take the time to walk there
   any more

And baby, you know I've got big plans
For that dangerous boat I've been dreamin' of
Novelty
Luxury
To count all the things that I do truly love

You have positively outdone yourself again, Lorraine
So delicious
Salacious
Magnificent
Indulgent
Gourmet
Lorraine, have you no shame?
Lorraine!

When you're that rich
Someone folds your cloths
Straightens your mess
The prince who learns to take care of himself
Will come to act
In his best interests

Do all rich kids become resourceful and industrious?
Do all rich kids become great humanitarians?
Uncommonly generous?
Ecologically conscientious?

Rich kids, prosperous
Rich kids, illustrious
In swimming pools with Rastafarians
Singing "The Star-Spangled Banner"
In the same hall with proud Aryans

Wouldn't spend no more time sweatin' rent
Low budget
Talk about mismanagement!
Hole in the bucket
Now!
This money
Someone tell me right now
Where is it?
Where was it spent, Goddammit!?

I go to work and slave for pay
Come back to this house every day
Roof over us
Paycheck to paycheck
Hand to mouth
Struggle continuous
Ten turned twenty
Twenty felled thirty
Should've got a license
Should've got a degree

Then we'll get a crazy TV
Bigger than you
Bigger than me
There'll even be a button
That makes commercials something you don't have
   to hear or see

Tye, the parolee
They picked him up in a limousine
Went straight to the city
Was he simply unlucky?
His friends … priorities
No, that's not *me*
Goin' back to the penitentiary
No!
That's not me!
That's not me!
Tye, the parolee

Then we can get the house painted
The kitchen upgraded
Hell we could *move!*
Then we could build
Stay thrilled
Travel

Snort gravel
In fine Italian shoes

We know you need somewhere to go
But y' can't pass through here
Last thanksgiving we held the can drive
At the spot where the levee broke
In Hurricane Guinevere
Would've fed everyone
Couldn't find a can opener anywhere

Fresh strawberries
Sweet mango
California grapefruit
Topsiders — Sperrys
Old money
Fresh loot

Then we could purchase
That exotic sportscar on display
"Looking good, Winthrop"
"Feeling good, Billy RAY"

A hobo reunion
On a cold, dark night

Worn shoes, shabby clothes, vacant stares
Toothlessness
Madness
Violence
A good fire blows away all cares

A solid gold steering wheel
For my two hands to drive
People like cocaine
Some live
Some are no longer alive

Then I'll buy me a Rembrandt
And some chewing gum
A Martin guitar
Built back in nineteen forty-one

I'll buy the world's biggest bag of Cracker Jacks
I'll buy a knapsack with new zippers and pleated
    reinforcements

Got no sour cream for my baked potato, honey
Hours ago I sent that boy to the store
With just enough money

The poor are tired of being poor
The human mind…
Only so much can it endure

It's shocking
A world with so much ghetto
Degraded men
Wounded women
Children's hearts
Old slogans, new lingo
John, Paul, George, and Ringo
Never played much around these parts

Even though we ain't got money
I'm so in love with ya, honey[11]
Laughter is the key to her heart[12]
"Where've y' been?
Wipe your nose
It's always runny
Weren't we gonna make a fresh start?"
Down *here* where it's always sunny

Yes I dine at the Forge
Nightly
That's my Tesla

That's my Bugatti
On Wednesday, I take the girls in my Bentley
Friday nights are for black Ferraris
They're parked out on the curb
Stay thirsty, friends
So swank, these illuminati
Yes, I could feed an island
For what they cost me
Yes, sir
A little something I've done for myself
Don't she scream?
Don't she purr?

Money is the root of all evil
Who hasn't heard that a thousand times?
A money tree
A money pit
Money made
Money lost
Money enough to pay these taxes
Money enough to pay these fines
A thousand times

A free bowl of soup
Black Friday
White Christmas

Discount offers
Coupons in the mail
Yes, we're going out of business
Scratch and dent sale
Volume! Volume!
Everything must go!

Will it fly?
Will it fall?
Shark tank blues
See the poor soul
Empty as a pocket
Empty as a pocket
With nothin' to lose

Big money, big sugar, big oil
Gambling
Pimping
Guns and stocks
Invest in security
Bodyguards and company
Molotov cocktails and rocks
Matchsticks and water cannons
Tear gas
Padlocks
Invest in security

See how quickly order drops
How do I feel?
I feel like a million bucks
Even though I'm shit out of luck somewhere *way*
    south of Carácas

Fortune is waiting to be kind
The Johnny Walker Black Label whiskey sign
"Just keep walking"
Me, myself, and I…
They'll be doing all the talking

Is it true
That less than one percent
Of the people got all the dough?
Everybody can't be as lucky as you, y' know

Money changes everything
I've got to learn that song
Is it about making ends meet?
Is it about not having what people need just to
    get along?
Is it about turning your back on a lover?
About rudely slammed doors?
Money changes everything
Cyndi Lauper by a trash can, 1984

That film came
With a-hundred-and-fifty-million-dollar price
Whats next in the cineplex?
I almost never think about 'em twice
At one point in time even Speilberg was a Hail Mary
   go-for-broke hit-or-miss roll of the dice

Don't pout
Find something to be happy about
Success
Yes, success
Wouldn't that be nice?
How to enter into the gates of paradise

Lord, won't you buy me a Mercedes Benz?
My friends all have Porsches
I must make amends

Yes I collect Food Stamps
And disability
My doctor said that's what I could do
I've got a small inheritance
My sisters have supported me since
The last job I held
Back in 1992
Or was it '93? Hate me!

You could say
That greed is a disease
Diseases spread
Listen…
Democracy don't rule the earth
You'd better get that in your head

Here's half the money
You have my every confidence, Sonny
Only a professional could do this job for me
We consider this a big favor
In the morning I'll meet you across the river
You can buy me a cup of coffee
We'll talk things over

I didn't have to stand and get free lunch
With skinny little Johnny Jones
I knew somehow that Sherry Sporn
Wasn't wearing designer clothes
George Velasquez's third-grade party
Was in a two-room apartment
The boulevard full of busy cars
Lay just beyond the pavement

Lu-Lu's Cornbread

I miss Lu-Lu's cornbread
I miss Lu-Lu's cornbread
I miss Lu-Lu's cornbread
I miss Lu-Lu's cornbread

I miss Lu-Lu's cornbread
I miss Lu-Lu's cornbread
I miss Lu-Lu's cornbread
I miss Lu-Lu's cornbread

I miss Lu-Lu's cornbread
I miss Lu-Lu's cornbread
I miss Lu-Lu's cornbread
I miss Lu-Lu's cornbread

100 Dollars in Miami Beach

With 100 dollars in Miami Beach,
You get a motel room renovated 30 years ago
With 100 dollars in Miami Beach
You get a 1-pound lobster, ice water, and 2 dinner rolls

The lock on the door had to be jimmied
The credit card machine didn't set
The people next door threw a tequila party
The rain kept up, half the week was wet

The lighting's so bad in the room
It kinda makes ya sick
Bathroom so small, to turn is to trip
"Honey wash your feet
Floor's got grit"

"Hello, operator?
This air conditioner in 103 sounds like something in
    it's broke
Please send up a fan"
The windows don't open
There's flaking paint
Could it be from a lead-based can?

Like in Puerto Rico or New Orleans
Y' wait to see another roach
100 dollars in Miami Beach,
The continental breakfast is just a rumor of black coffee and toast

For 100 dollars in Miami Beach
The walls are marked from days before
Bed felt like a cot
Great view of the alley I got!
There were channels on the TV, but not a lot
It's gettin' on four
It's bad out there
That's what I checked in here for

100 dollars in Miami Beach
Gets ya a woman climbin' a pole
Cartier, Romero Britto
Families at 'The Frieze' ice cream parlor window

100 dollars in Miami Beach,
You can buy your buddies a beer
Y' say y' never heard of a $9 Heineken?
Well it's now $12, friend
$9 was *last year*

For 100 dollars in Miami Beach…
She's made up, but clearly unkempt
The ancient street sweeper on 7th street finally died
All the store owners openly wept

7½ million people
In some kind of sweated tizzy
This is not the Deep South
This is a borough of old New York City

So humid…
Is it always this way?
Africa hot
Walk around the block
You need a change of clothing
And the Dolphins haven't been in the playoffs
Since Dan Marino was in Texas stadium when it was snowing

With a 100 dollar bill, sir
Take a boat ride past the stars' backyards
Some of the celebrities' kids have BB guns
And they'll get ya, the little bastards
(I met Gloria Estefan
When she smiles, you think of the sun)

Anything can happen here, and often does
Don't get drunk before you get a tattoo
"Are you alright?" The artist asks
You're turning white
You're turning green
You're turning blue
And you know what that trash can's for
Sittin' right beside you

Uh-oh
Here comes the fuzz
"Sir, do you know why I stopped you?"
"Yes officer, I do"
If there's a way to make a dollar in Miami Beach
A dollar will be made
On Ocean Drive, Collins, or Washington Avenue

Gotta pay the toll on 75, 27, and Route 1
Amtrack
Grayhound
The Friendly Skies…
Not a mountain or a hill till the state of
   Georgia comes

For 100 dollars in Miami Beach
Trickle down 'Freakonomics'

Glass in the cut
Cut in the glass
Nah, dew sweet from high canopy green mountain mist
But garbage
Jersey Turnpike trash

A hundred dollars in Miami Beach
Gets you a consultation with a plastic surgeon
Plastic surgeons in Iowa
They don't live in the same fashion
Style, style
Style and fashion
Style and fashion
Style and fashion

I know where to go in Miami
Where you can sit in peace
And feel something real
Here, a week goes by pretty much in seven days
The ocean has a bathtub feel

Politics
Tow truck grips
Homelessness
A rapper on every corner
For 100 dollars you can hire a barbershop quartet

Flower for the lady?
Cigar for the gent?
Angelo Dundee used to train his grunts right here
   on this corner

British tourist families
Like walking pink cotton candy
Wanna know what it's like to drive a fine Italian
   sports car?
Why sure! Come on, Henry!

100 dollars in Miami Beach
Take in a movie
Read the paper
Sip a daring cup of coffee
There's a golf course running down the middle of
   the island
Let's go burn down a tree!
I ain't runnin' for mayor
Don't matter to me
(But please … not the Australian pine
Their needles rouse and haunt the breeze)
Spooky, sublime

100 dollars in Miami Beach goes pretty quickly
If summer thunder rumbles close

There's lightning in your vicinity

Paris Hilton said, "Miami is *icky*"
There's a speedboat in Billy Joel's backyard
He named it *Liberty*
The speedboats in Miami move awfully quickly

100 dollars in Miami Beach
Legs all the way down to the ground
It's quite a scene
Snowbirds from Canada everywhere
Little black dress cuisine

"*Cafe con leche…*
Y platanos cinnamon
La ropa vieja
¡Arlene!
¡Mi comida…!
¿Cuando?
¡Arlene!"
"*!Cayate, niño!*
Son personas en mi culo!
No trabajo solamente portigo!"
"*Lo siento*
Sin problema, Arlene, mi amor"

100 dollars in Miami Beach
You won't wish you'd gone to Aspen
100 dollars in Miami Beach
"Henry, open this sucker up
Let's see what she'll do
We're on vacation!

Saying for Kelly Clarkson

What doesn't kill you makes you stronger?
No…
What doesn't kill you *can* kill you
And eventually will

WALK IT OFF, SID

What if your mind didn't go back to sober?
What if 'wound up' didn't unwind?
Balance…?
Over
His breathing is shallow
And his color…!
You'd be lookin' for an out of some kind

What if your mind got caught in the shock?
No way of stirring the flesh in the pot?
You've been over the top
Y' know how it feels
Another chance, another shot
Junkie rut
Hell on wheels

Are there people out there with devastated minds
Making music of the non-musical kind?
Mouthwash

Absinthe

Sterno

Glue

It's a goddamn shame that a musical instrument can be held by the likes of you

Are there people out there with devastated minds?
Untreated by doctors?
Unattended by guards?
Here's your hour of sunshine
Devastated
You ate the whole bag at once?
Yeah … and I wasn't the same for months

In the open doorway
A hideous young man
A cheap motel hallway
Lights flickerin'
He took a half-step in
Dilated loser
A meth monster
Stood my ground
Knife's on the dresser

A life can become a sack of wickedness
Fixes and tricks comin' out of the sticks
Spun…
Spun-ness
Never no more on the ball
'Spun-ness'
The cold-blooded

And their 'fun-ness'
The addled
Seething
Icy and mean
The pathos of these pitiful
They're on their own favorite team

They get more brave at night
A fool in the passenger seat with a gun
Senseless
Violence
Random
Boredom
I'm sorry, but what is "scum?"

They who have no peace
Was peace denied them?
Spare the rod
Spoil the child
I wasn't hit
I don't hit them
(And that's no way to talk to your children)

What if your mind didn't go back to sober
Better get up and walk it off, Sid

Seems the only thing you didn't figure out
Was how long you had to live
And wasn't that last line just plain stupid?

Balance?
Over
Life *was* a four-leaf clover
There's your out of some kind
Better get up and walk it off, Sid
You don't know; this could be the last time

HEY, YEAH…

Hey yeah, do these drunks hold for one another
Any lasting appeal?
She's sittin' there wonderin' 'bout
The next useless thing he's gonna reveal

You can sense her embarrassment at being there
Embarrassed for herself
Embarrassed for Joe
Deeply depressed in increments
One day she'll live in another zipcode

It is said in Genesis that woman is cursed
Because it is man she desires
He's workin' too hard to get the job done
Of closeness
Fires don't put out fires

Double Jägermeister and the surf and turf
Well, aren't you just the "Wreck of the
    Edmund Fitzgerald?"
It'll be Christmas in what? 13 weeks?
I got a drum
You know any carols?

Baltimore was Closed

Stayed at the Harlem 'Y' this time
135th Street
Renovated
Thoroughly modern loo
TV
Little fridge, too
Looking out at New York's century skyline

Every tile in place
Clean and well kept
Stayed 3 nights
Swam two times
82 degrees
Nicely heated
(None of the Village People were there)

All the churches needed pressure washing
On both the Madison and 6th Avenue sides
You can catch a cab in New York City
But you're not goin' anywhere…
I tried

Bussed to DC from New Orleans
Baltimore was closed

Poor folks use Greyhound bus lines
Someone's always snoring so loud
Y' wanna punch 'em in the nose

Outside of Nashville one time
A singer was on board
Her name was Stanton…
Ricki Stanton
I heard her talking business with someone
I asked her if she'd sing one
It was sweet in the dark
You'd think I'd remember what she sung
The driver didn't tell her to "pipe down"
Stanton
Pretty Black woman
Singin' on a Greyhound bus out of Nashville town

They were officers of the law
And they broke that boy's spinal cord
They broke that boy in Baltimore
Broke him
They huddled up
Then they shamed themselves

News said he had a rap sheet down to the floor
Never to walk a step more

They shamed themselves…
That's it and nothing else
Legs draggin'
Back saggin'

Is this America behind closed doors?
Never thought this could happen
Baltimore's finest
The finest of Baltimore
Without the police and governor
Men, each other would devour

Alcohol
Tobacco
Narcotics
Firearms
Kids in school uniforms
Pigs' feet in red jars
Dirty floor
Broken tiles
Del Monte in syrup
Chips Ahoy!
Blemished oranges
Bruised Apples
"Mama, I want a Snapple"
"Hush up…

Shut your mouth, boy"
The only thing good about the scene
Was that it was that time of the morning…
When the Scotch tape on the store front
Mixes with the dust in the sunbeams pouring in

They showed Crazy some cash
They gave Crazy a gun
And they told him what to do…
Other than fighting the police
Find something *else* to do

The cop Crazy killed
Wouldn't he have done some good?
Like his father before him
Who'd retired from the force
Blue suits in jungle neighborhoods
His kid in a hat on the first base line
The next game day at Yankee Stadium

Arthur McDuffie
Remember him?
Smoke over a Black Sox game in '66 or '67
Celebrating over Reginald Denny
Got one; like to get plenty
Your innocent victim

Black folk riot
Burn the fucker down
CVS won't rebuild
Whole Foods Market skipped Overtown

Poverty
Black like you isn't white like me
It's a fairy tale
Can't you see?
Poor forever
Underqualified
Shamefully
Painfully
Reading level: grade three
It's true
Know what I's sayin'?
I'm aksin' ya?
Know what I mean?
F'n'a let ya know
Need anythin'?

Can't read
Opportunities
It's called "Welfare"
From Washington DC
What year?

Must've been in the 60s
To give those who ain't got a little more[13]
They're *poor*
That's the real situation
Violation upon violation

But if you've got the notion
You can score down the street
Up the steps
Knock twice
Then two quick raps on the door
Junkie, you've been classified
There's a label next to your name
There's a cop or two in the precinct
You won't walk away from quite the same

This is how you think
This is what your future enlists
For the disenfranchised
With no training or education enough
To take part in any opportunity
That already hardly exists

Have you ever looked into the face of a
    homeless person?

Got close enough to someone on
    permanent excursion?
Out in all that heat
Facing the cold
Hungry
Thirsty
Nasty
Sadly muttering his case of old
A doctor
A brilliant lawyer
An actor
An artist
When your intellect starts to work against you
You're well on the road to *finished*

Kicked to the curb
Disheveled
Sick
And a blanket is all he has up against it

"Let me see your report card"
"Don't you have homework?"
"Turn down that radio"
  Too much o' nothin'
  Is nothin' t' do

And nowhere to go
Gym suit heroes
To be taken most seriously…
By any means necessary
"You don't have to do this!"
But he does
He's Mr. Legendary
Pretty scary
Really scary

What have we got in common, you and me?
I gave at the office
You are your own unfolding story
You're on the streets?
How very sad
Can't find shelter
We're very sorry

Spirituals
Gospel
Blues
Jazz and *this*…?
Dick Clark
Cornelius

Life ain't a bowl of cherries
Life isn't summer camp
Oh the frightful things a school bag carries
Ain't got a quarter for a postage stamp

Oh the things a school bag carried
When you were young
And your life was an open book[14]
Of maps
Mathematics
Erasers
Thumbtacks
Hit records
Hard facts
Gym pants
Calculators
Plays with three acts
A flute
A clarinet
A sax
A bus pass
Papers
Pens
The Periodic Table

Paperbacks
Sweat socks
Adidas
20 bags o' somethin'
My boys 'r' lookin' f' me in the halls between class

FULL OF YOURSELF

For Rosie, Jen, Paula, and Esther

Aren't you just so full of yourself?
Prob'ly what I thought of you when we first met
Isn't he just so full of himself…?
Well, they say you should go with the first
   impression set

What room in the house might this country be?
Chicken bone sandwich in the kitchen
Crime scene tape wrapped around the TV

Aren't you just so full of yourself?
Well, if you love anything, it's the sound of your
   own voice
But aren't you just so full of yourself?
As if any merry prankster ever really had a choice

What room in the house might this country be?
What shape is the roof in?
Yes, when it's raining

Yes, I feel like I'm the only pebble
   on the beach

Always one step closer to knowing
I'm still in one piece

When I first met you, baby
I thought you were one of those fellas who's just so full of himself
Yeah, well, some of us might start to reaching early along the way
Oh, so very full of yourself…
Well, I've come to think that some things could be up to me, someday

What room in the house might this country be?
Are there posters on the walls?
Are there black-light transparencies?

Oh yes, I know him
And I can tell you he's nothing but full of himself
Thinks the ground starts to shakin' somewhere on the Earth
Every time he opens his mouth
I don't take him seriously at all
Fool's just so full of himself
I hear he's broke
I hear he's sick

He's C.I.A
He's sloth

What room in the house might this country be?
I've got a smoking jacket on
I believe this glass holds brandy

I feel like I've got to make my prayers known unto
    the sun
Now how d' you go about doin' that?
Gentlemen? Anyone?

So full of myself
The cult of personality
So full of myself
Death by gravity
What room in the house might this country be?
I don't live here
I just clean and do laundry

Aren't you just so full of yourself?
My, you haven't changed at all
So full of yourself
Convenience store company
One and all

One and all
What room in the house might this country be?
Trap doors in floors
Labyrinth
Secrecy

Yes, I feel like the lone banyan tree
Reaching out with my limbs so spookily
At the far side of the park
I love it when a couple comes
And scratches their initials in my bark

Yes, I'm full of myself
The whole trip is capability
Full of myself
Potential and evermore potentiality

What room?
On such a rainy day
How nice…
A cup of tea
Do it yourself if you want it done properly
… I'm *full* of myself, baby
And yeah, the laughs are with me

I'm so glad I've got somewhere to be
I'm so glad to be part of a remedy
So glad the cathedral's intact
Dear me
A jubilee!
And nobody invited me?
Thought you were my friends
Bunch o' hacks!

The Collection

If you don't have a million dollars
You don't own a fine Italian sports car
If you don't have a million dollars
You don't pay for drinks at the Fountainbleau Bar

Las Vegas, it ain't the greatest
And you're not 18 years old
This world can make you mean
This world can turn you cold

If you ain't got a million dollars,
Your breakfast isn't ready
If you ain't got a million dollars
You drink the stuff that makes a man's hands unsteady

Las Vegas ain't the greatest
They're always too young
And you're always too old
This world is making you mean
This world is turning you cold

Someone's doing dishes
Someone's sweeping floors
What's a sweetheart like you ever come here for?

Las Vegas ain't the greatest
It's bust, bluff, or fold
This world is making you mean
This world is turning you cold

If you ain't got a million dollars,
You can still feel like a millionaire
You can make your blood as thick as gold
Powdered perfume in the air

Las Vegas ain't the greatest
The menus are freezing cold[15]
And for some reason when you leave Las Vegas
Nothing's s'posed to be told

Look at them long legs
They go all the way down to the ground
Oh boy, don't it take your breath away?
Don't it make your heart pound?

Las Vegas ain't the greatest
It's a *Penthouse* centerfold
This world is making you mean
This world is turning you cold

The Ferrari
The Corvette
The Maserati, better yet
One vintage green Pantera
And for you, my Farrah…
A long, dark blue Bentley
An original white '82 Countach Lamborghini
You've been so good to me, sweetie

So let's see…

Sing for me now, baby
I'll tip you all the way through Junior College
You've got a body that came out of a bottle, out of a vase
You've got more than a few good plums left on the tree
What tree?
I'll tell you
The tree of good and evil
The Luxor
Caesar's
The Sands
The Mirage
Honey, the tree of good and evil
Darlin', the tree of knowledge

Willie said
"The secret to happiness is
Fast horses
Younger women
Old whisky
And more money"
51 states in the union
Willie Nelson
Always a gentleman
Always will be

If you ain't got a million dollars
Your breakfast isn't ready

Saying from a prayer book

To momentarily acknowledge
That our physical selves are capable of ecstasy
How you would labor
To take care of it all
What barriers would serve to honor this blessed state?
Well, there's stuff each society and culture erects
To eventually trample

Y' Know What I Like About You?

Y' know what I like about you?
I like your sweet voice
When you've slept the whole night through
And y' know what I like about you?
You smile back at me
When I can't help but smile at you

When you take off your glasses
There's someone I never knew
What I like about you
It's like all you can be is true
I'm yet to meet a woman who — thank God! — didn't
  prove a little loose
You're a kid skippig around, laughing in a dress stained
  with grape juice

What I like about you
You're adorable
I adore you
And you stay right with me, right on cue
We may not be perfect, but who is?
Who?

To appreciate what counts
To rejoice and be grateful
Hey Jude

What do I like about you?
I'm James Dean sneakin' up on Natalie Wood
Debra Winger tips her chin in a grin
To stay right where we are...
Till there's sounds of healin'
Deeper breathin'
Good lovin'...
Oh, what a feelin'

What I like, *really* like about you, cuz
You speak Spanish like a white girl does
Your French is something, too
You hear just what you wanna hear
Like all women do
After all this time
I'm still glad to be with you
New Hampshire, thick socks, hiking shoes
We'll take out a jar and tap a tree or two
Me and you

You don't fly off the cuff
Enough is enough

Someone could really love you
What I like about you
You're from the south
Maryland 'll do
Folk dance is the only dance you've done
Or 'll ever do
I'm moved to apologize when I can't change my mood
A lighthouse stands with its base kinda wide
Bright light shinin' through

Did we really sit for hours out on Española Way?
I had somewhere else to be
But they could all go away
The flowery scent from the laundry
Sure was a beautiful day
We lacked for nothing to say
You're the prayer I won't let myself pray…

Was this boy made for you
And this girl for me?
Dark curly hair
Didn't you tell me it was straight until your 28th year?
I'd better end this song
Before it becomes too much to hear
You don't wanna go to any rock 'n' roll show
Baby, you're so square

But I don't care[16]
My life felt like a consolation prize…
With you, no more
And that's not just cheap sentiment
Honest, Shel, don't we think alike?
Don't we jibe together?

Greenland
Iceland
Ireland
England
Land Ho!
Behold
That's me and you, Shel
Passin' by the rock of Gibraltar
Can you believe it?
Yes…
No…

I could never write a love song
The way it's meant to be
I've never walked and talked in old England
What a trip that would be
We'll rent us a convertible, baby
Yeah, an MGB

No, a Jaguar XKE!
Don't forget your scarf and goggles, m'lady

Sshhh
Oh, me!
Shelley, please
I'm no stranger
I know what it is
From more than recklessness and danger
Your daughter's doin' fine
The clothes are in the drawers
Lunch is packed
The dog's out back
Is there gas in the car?
Yes, there's gas in the car[17]

How long has it taken me
To know and believe
That you're not another ninny
With something up her sleeve?
Sshhh
It's only me!
Shelley please

20 Reasons NOT to go to your 30th High School Reunion

21) I guess I've got a few gray hairs, and I reckon I've balded some, too. *Y'think?*
20) I had my mind set on losing 20 pounds but I didn't lose 5, 10, 15, or 20.
    I had my mind set on losing 20 pounds…
    But I didn't lose any.
19) The nineteenth reason: We are the ugly Americans, too.
18) It seems like the purest act of masochism you could ever drum up.
17) Nobody knows the trouble I've seen — *nobody*
16) What can I tell ya? Life got in the way
15) I still live in the same 750-square foot apartment only 10 minutes from here.
14) I'm not going to my high school reunion if Tom Petty and the Heartbreakers are playing anywhere within a 650-mile radius of here.
13) I'm too busy studying my Chinese.
12B) If I get drunk, I'll be miserable and helpless, and bumpity-bump; what starts making perfect sense?

12) I embarrassed myself on more than one occasion in high school. Oh please remind me; every 10 years I'll take my fair share of abuse

11) My high school sweetheart became a marathon runner. She has run around the entire globe cumulatively more than 17 times— while you and I ate potato chips.

10) The tenth reason not to go to your 30th high school reunion: We're probably gonna hear "Rapper's Delight."

9) And Loverboy's "Everybody's working for the weekend." Christ!

8B) I'll just blow if off and order Domino's….. "Oh look, The Royal Tannenbaums is on again."

8) Acaremas danyol san. Benihana Arigato.

7B) Pam Strahl wore those white shiny pants to the Starlight Room at our 20th reunion. Maybe she'll wear them again…?

7) Wanna see my tattoos again?

6) In anticipation of being here with you all … I stopped taking my psychotropic re-uptake inhibitors 6½ days ago. Oh my God!

5) I'm just looking for a kiss.

4) You're all highly imperfect and deeply flawed, but not me!

3) Amy said, "Yes, I'm married, but not tonight!"
2B) Will it all be like a strange dream where we wake up the next morning knowing our true age?

The number two reason:
2) Hey man; I thought you were dead…

And number one of the 20 reasons not to go to your 30th High School Reunion:
1) Nobody ever loved me there, anyway!

LET'S SEE, A BAND...

Do I need a whacked out guitarist
To bend that killer chord?
Or do I need someone who plays *Kinda Blue*
Reserved

I need a rubber-band hollow-body jazz guitar
And a big stand-up bass
Played with a cello's bow
Everybody here gets a brand new car
So long as you lend your ear and tap your toe
Oh yeah! An Epiphone!

Popcorn
A popcorn drummer
Makes me feel so *alive*
Set him straight, he'll be a regular full-blooded
Encore guy
Live!

That bass player
Derby hat, will travel
Now you see me
Now you don't

Of course, I keep that stand-up ready and reliable
And more 'n once been down this same road

Some of these Mississippi boys
They plugged in
And on and on they went to play
Those bluegrass boys, that Georgia clay
'Foggy Mountain Breakdown' on a one-string
'Dueling Banjos,' 'Feuding Banjos'
Whatever ya call it
It's their thing, their *thang*

Listen to that organ
He could play for The Dead on New Year's Eve
Number 1 Heartbreaker: Benmont Tench
Professor Roy Bittan and Phantom Dan Federici
That B-3 bleeding seaweed all in the weave
(Yeah, I used to get stoned with Bruce Springsteen
And his buddy, Miami Steve)

A choir
I am a member of a choir, I'm sure of it
I've been a member of a choir for years
I raise my voice in song
Over landlords, neighbors, and peers

Mad!
So let's see…
2 guitars, bass, drums
Piano
Choir
Choice!
I'm going to Nashville
Find some ferocious sons o' bitches
They're the ones you wanna hire
Here's my best Johnny Cash voice

How 'bout a horn section?
Keep it sparse
Sparse 'til the walls come down
Let the trumpets brawl in the trombones' breakdown
With a saxophone prowlin' around

There's this jam band out of San Francisco
Used to play a song called "Built to Last"
There's a horn solo over the middle
It's royal; it's got royalty
It's stately without bein' stately
Branford Marsalis on stage with the cast
Of the Grateful Dead
Big moments

Skill

Talent

Let's see ... a band!

END NOTES

Yeah, Dumb!

1. (p.28) It was twelve o'clock when I realized I was having no fun
   —John Prine. *Illegal Smile.*

2. (p.29) Don't hand me no lines and keep your hands to yourself
   —Georgia Satellites. *Keep Your Hands to Yourself.*

Somethin' Else to Me

3. (p.38) And the skyline of Toronto is something you'll get onto … live there for a while
   —Gordon Lightfoot. *Alberta Bound.*

4. (p.41) You may be a rock 'n' roll addict … women in a cage
   —Bob Dylan. *Gotta Serve Somebody.*

5. (p.45) Well it sounds so sweet … moon went down
   —Chuck Berry. *Around and Around.*

6. (p.46) Everybody here ... dancin' in the moonlight
   —King Harvest. *Dancin' in the Moonlight.*

My Bob Dylan
7. (p.69) "A fine working ... money machine"
   —Jorma Kaukonen. *Prohibition.*

Talking Shit
8. (p.106) I didn't write 'em for that, but I ..."
   —Bob Dylan interview

Their Biggest Worry
9. (p.110) From morning till night ... hustle
   —Bob Dylan. *Under the Red Sky.*

Iggy Pop
10. (p.114) Ladies are unwell ... gentlemen vomit.
    —Dir. by Richard Benjamin. *My Favorite Year.*

Then We Can
11. (p.131) Even though we ain't got money, I'm so in love with ya, honey
    —Anne Murray. *Danny's Song.*

12.   (p.131) Laughter is the key to her heart
— Crosby, Stills & Nash. *Suite Judy Blue Eyes.*

Baltimore was Closed

13. (p.160) To give those who ain't got …
— Bruce Hornsby. *That's Just the Way it is.*

14. (p.163) When you were young and your life was an open book…
— Paul McCartney. *Live and Let Die.*

The Collection

15. (p.172) The menus are freezing cold
— Tom Waits. *The Piano Has Been Drinkin.*

Y' Know What I Like About You

16. (p.180) Baby, you're so square, but …
— Elvis Presley. *You're So Square.*

17. (p.181) Is there gas in the car? Yes, there's gas in the car.
— Steely Dan. *Kid Charlemagne.*

www.ingramcontent.com/pod-product-compliance
Lightning Source LLC
Chambersburg PA
CBHW031144160426
43193CB00008B/244